Introduction

It's sometimes easy for couples to be stuck in their own worlds and only focus on themselves. Spending some time together each day is important to keep the couple's relationship strong, but it only works if the two get to communicate and share their thoughts with each other. This is important for any relationship to thrive.

Activity such as asking your partner questions about what they do during the day or asking them what their hopes and dreams are for the future, is easy and takes little effort to accomplish. The more you know about your partner, the more you'll feel like you understand them and that both of you are on the same page.

Asking your partner questions about themselves will help you learn more about who they really are as an individual. You'll want to know how to make them smile when they are down, how to make them laugh when they are in a bad mood, or what will make your spouse feel loved by you. Being curious about who they are as an individual can help strengthen your relationship and enjoy a deeper sense of intimacy with them.

Questions in This Book

This book comprises questions that are thought provoking and may not be the easiest questions to answer. Questions that require deep thinking are beneficial in helping you understand who your partner is, and it will help to strengthen the relationship between both of you.

Staying true with one another is an important part of keeping the relationship healthy and asking questions to know each other better can help keep this goal a reality.

There's no doubt that it takes a lot of effort and patience to ask your partner difficult questions about themselves, but the positive things that come from this effort are well worth it in the end. You'll be able to build a better connection between each other because you'll understand each other more than before, making all aspects of your relationship stronger as a result.

How to Use This Book

Method 1:
There are 100 questions for you to ask your partner. You'll want to pick out a handful each day, so that the two of you will have something new and interesting to talk about at dinner time. This way, it won't become too overwhelming or difficult for either of you to handle.

Make sure that both of you are prepared with questions (so pick your question in advance) before going into this activity, because it's not good to be the only person asking questions all night long.

Method 2:
One person picks and answers a question, then the other person will have to answer that question and do the same in a new question, on a separate occasion.

Both will write their answer to the questions in their respective HER and HIM section.

This method is wonderful because there is no time pressure and allows one enough space to reflect on the questions before answering them. This will bring about more meaningful conversations once the question is answered.

Activity Tips

It's advisable that there should be no extra distractions at home when working through this book, such as people or pets running around in the house. This can distract and may cause one of you to lose focus on answering those questions. You'll want to make sure that both of you know how to stay calm and focused so that the activity will work well for you.

It's also a good idea to do this activity when there are no friends and family members around. This allows your partner to be able to open up about themselves without feeling embarrassed in front of anyone else because it's just the two of you being exposed. So make sure that everyone has gone home for the night before starting this workbook together.

One thing you'll want to remember when going through this book together is that there are no 'right' or 'wrong' answers, but just personal preference. If your partner has trouble answering a question, then they are free to say "I don't know" if they can't come up with an answer immediately.

Token of Love Keepsake

You can write or doodle your thoughts and answers to make it fun and interesting. Once both of you have completed this book, it can serve as the best souvenir that you can ever have.

HER

If you had a choice between going on the best date of your life with me or getting $50,000 right now, which would you choose and why?

HIM

HER

If we were stranded on an island and could only have 3 items with us, what would they be? Why?

HIM

We're at a party and there are 10 people in our group of friends. How many of them do you feel comfortable enough to socialize with me around (ie: talk freely about just about anything)?

HER

Would you rather give up all TV for a year or give up your cell phone for a month? Why?

HIM

HER

If we had a child together, who he/she should look like the most and whose physical features our child should inherit mostly from both of us?

HIM

HER

What 3 things do I do regularly that annoy you the most? Why do they annoy you? Be honest!

HIM

HER

If you could discover any new fact about your life, what would it be? What past event would you want me to explain in more detail to clarify something that happened between us?

HIM

HER

Which is better: Homemade coffee or Starbucks coffee? Why?

HIM

HER

Have I done anything lately that has made you feel very proud of me where you've told others about it afterwards? If so, tell me the story and why you were proud.

HIM

HER

Tell me the top 10 things I do that make our relationship strong and happy!

HIM

HER

Which part of our relationship would you change if a genie gave you 3 wishes?

HIM

HER

If we could see into our future, what would be the 3 things that will make it the most successful 10 years from now?

HIM

HER

We've been together for a few years now and you know me better than almost anyone. If there's one thing that makes it hard to live with me, what is it? Are there any ways that I can improve in this regard?

HIM

HER

What do you think are the 3 things that are important to me in a relationship (doesn't need to be about love, just anything special)?

HIM

HER

What's the biggest issue facing our relationship right now that we are going to have to face? How are we going to handle it, and what do you think will be the results if we don't make any changes by then?

HIM

HER

If I was trapped on a deserted island with no one else around but you for an entire month, how would you show me that your feelings for me never changed from before?

HIM

HER

If a stranger knew nothing about us as a couple, would you be proud to introduce me and tell others that I am your significant other? Why or why not?

HIM

HER

What's the biggest secret that you would like to share with me after being this long in this relationship (it can be anything!)

HIM

HER

Have there been any times where we both committed an error which caused a rift between us, and if so, what was it and, most importantly, how are we going to fix it so that it doesn't happen again?

HIM

HER

What does our relationship mean to you? Why is our relationship special to you? Does it fulfill a purpose in your life or someone else's life?

HIM

HER

Have there been any major events happened in our lives during the past year (doesn't need to be just bad things) How did they affect me on a personal level (those close to me I mean) and how will they affect you in the next 5 years if we don't do something to change?

HIM

HER

When we are having a disagreement with each other, talking about our feelings, why should I keep my cool or chill out before we start fighting?

HIM

HER

How can I prove to you how much love molds us together and becomes inseparable friends forever?

HIM

HER

How would your life be worse off if we were never
friends/dated? Explain why.

HIM

HER

What are 3 things you always enjoy doing with me when we spend time together (or just something else you like about me as a person)?

HIM

HER

Please talk about one of your goals or resolutions which will help us grow closer or strengthen our relationship (doesn't have to be directly about our relationship, just something that will make life better or more interesting for us)

HIM

If you could have any superpower in the world, what would it be and how would it affect me? (or why did you choose this one?) Explain your answer.

HER

How do you think we've changed most from the first day we met to now? What are 3 things that annoy you about me now but didn't before we started dating?

HIM

HER

I believe that being on time is very important in everyday life, whether it's work, school, social events, etc. What is something that you can do to help me be more on time? What is something that I can do to help you be more on time?

HIM

HER

What is your favorite song that we listen to together? Why do you like it so much and what does the song mean to us as a couple in relationship terms?

HIM

HER

If someone gave me an apple for every time they told me why they love me, how many apples would I have at the end of my life by having this person with me forever?

HIM

HER

Is there something you need to tell me (that is not too personal) but once you say it will make your relationship with me stronger and better in the future?

HIM

HER

If we could go to any restaurant in the world for dinner, where would it be and why?

HIM

HER

What is one of the greatest strengths you have as a person and why?

HIM

HER

Was there a point in time where I made an impression on you, but then it changed after spending more time with me (like if at first you thought I was funny but then didn't think so anymore)?

HIM

HER

Complete this phrase: I'm so glad we met because _____.
Why?

HIM

HER

What is the best vacation we have ever had and why?

HIM

Do you feel like our relationship succeeds or fails based on the type of people we are when together rather than what goes right or wrong between us at any given time, and is there anything about my personality that makes you think otherwise?

HER

Is it easier for you to see yourself with someone else romantically instead of me because I'm not someone else (like one of your childhood friends, close relatives or a celebrity)?

HIM

HER

What would be your ideal date night?

HIM

HER

Do you feel that our expectations of each other contradict one another, like if I want us to spend time together more than you. Please explain.

HIM

HER

Tell me what it is that will get us through times when people say things about us that aren't true. How can we spend more time with those who are saying good things instead? Please explain.

HIM

HER

What's something that you really want to do before you depart from this world (and can probably achieve very soon)?

HIM

HER

If I asked your friends right now to describe what kind of person you are, would they say nice things or mean things, and why might this be?

HIM

HER

If you could change anything about our relationship, what would it be? Please explain.

HIM

HER

Are there any words that I've said or done that truly hurt you more than anything else, even if it was an accident on my part? Please elaborate.

HIM

HER

What is something important that everyone should know about us (such as how we're trustworthy or just live our lives well)? Please explain.

HIM

HER

When I think of all the time and energy that's gone into our relationship so far, what value can I add to make everything better between us?

HIM

HER

Have you ever had a dream that involved us being together in some way? If yes, explain the dream and how we were connected.

HIM

HER

Is there something that makes me less likely than most people to be happy in a long-term relationship (such as being too judgmental of others, not thinking I can trust them after someone hurt me before)? Please explain.

HIM

HER

Is our relationship less likely to last because of how we relate to each other (like if I don't see what others think about us or value their opinions too little)? Please explain.

HIM

HER

If we were living together somewhere besides where we live now, do you think either of us would be less likely to thrive and be happy in that living situation than most other people are? Please explain.

HIM

HER

Is there something about how I treat you that would make anyone else think less of me if they knew? Please explain.

HIM

Do you think there's anything at all wrong with me as a person, and if so, what is it? Please explain.

HER

If I asked your friends if we're a suitable match for each other, would they say yes or no and why might this be?

HIM

HER

Would you accept a compromise as being an effective way of solving problems between us when needed, and is there anything that wouldn't work as a compromise between us? Please explain.

HIM

Do you think there's a difference between relationship partners and marriage partners, and if so, what is that difference? Please explain.

HER

Are there any serious changes that we should make as a
couple, or are there just things about us that need to be
more consistent (like our goals and morality)? Please explain.

HIM

HER

What's the best thing I've done for you as a partner? What would I do differently if I could change 1 thing in my past behavior towards you? Please explain.

HIM

HER

If we had children together, how would it affect our relationship down the road (and what can we learn now so that we can avoid those problems)?

HIM

HER

If I were to give advice to another person who was thinking about being with you, what would I say?

HIM

HER

In the long run, what would I say that you should do or not do with your life? How can I show you how we're constantly on the same wavelength–especially when it comes to relationships? Please explain.

HIM

HER

If there is 1 thing that I'm willing to change for you, what will your request be?

HIM

HER

How can I help you feel more loved in the way that's right for someone who has done so much in a relationship? Please explain.

HIM

HER

How would I know when to leave a relationship if things no longer work for us?

HIM

HER

What's 1 thing we shouldn't do with other friends that can make our relationship seem less valuable than others? Please explain.

HIM

HER

How can I make you feel loved by others when you deserve so much more treatment than that (such as parents, siblings or friends not treating you well enough)? Please explain.

HIM

HER

If I asked your opinion about someone who was interested in me romantically, what would you say? Please explain.

HIM

HER

Are there any quiet times between us where I should be giving more attention to you, or is there something else I should be doing (like spending time with others separately)? Please explain.

HIM

HER

How do you feel about changes we've made to get along better as a couple? What else can we do?

HIM

HER

Is there anything special that I could do for you annually (such as a holiday, birthday or anniversary) that is so meaningful to you?

HIM

HER

What do I need to know about your friends/family that will help me be a more effective partner for you (and therefore them)? Please explain.

HIM

HER

Do you think there's any way in which my past experiences are keeping us from getting closer today? Please explain.

HIM

HER

If I could change one thing in myself that seems like it would be the most difficult, what would it be? Please explain.

HIM

HER

How can I make you feel loved by me starting now so that we have a better chance of spending time with others together in the future (such as family members or special friends)?
Please explain.

HIM

HER

Is there anything special you'd need to know about me to trust me enough to invite others over more often (such as suspicion, worrying about my safety or jealousy)?

HIM

HER

What do I need to do for you right now so that people view us favorably when we're out somewhere together (like showing up on time and being well-dressed instead of sleepy and messy)?

HIM

HER

What's 1 thing we've done together that could be a model for others in the future?

HIM

HER

How did I make you feel when we first met? Do these feelings continue till now? Can you describe the emotions if they are different from before?

HIM

Does my personality make it harder for me to find love romantically than most people (like if I'm too critical, judgmental, controlling in the way I interact with others)? Please explain.

HER

Do you think your family would be prouder of me if they knew how we treat each other instead of just knowing how well our relationship is working on paper?

HIM

HER

What's 1 thing about our relationship that makes people jealous of us? Your explanation behind this feeling or emotion for each person would be really helpful too.

HIM

HER

How would you visualize how life will be if we were to switch our role today?

HIM

HER

What can I do (or what can we do together) so I wouldn't feel pressured by you into changing something about myself or our relationship with each other because of issues from your past that I'm not responsible for? Please explain.

HIM

HER

If we were able to be together forever, would it be in a way that seems fair and supportive for both of us? Please explain.

HIM

HER

What's 1 thing about the idea of me coming back to life after we depart from this world that you're curious about?

HIM

HER

Tell me about a few of the people who have meant a lot to you in your life and how they helped you. What did they do for you?

HIM

HER

Tell me about one way I've made things better for you lately or done something special that didn't involve money. Please explain.

HIM

HER

What's the most important thing that we can do together right now, but are not because of negligence or selfishness on either part?

HIM

HER

Do you think it's all worth it (going through this process with me)? Why or why not?

HIM

HER

Is there anything else that would bring our relationship to the next level, and last forever, and be as happy as possible?

HIM

HER

What is something I should stop doing to improve our relationship? Please explain.

HIM

HER

Is there a struggle going on between us right now that nobody knows about but could become public or get bigger within the next month? Please share details.

HIM

HER

Is there anything you want to say to me that would make this relationship better for the both of us, or are you worried that saying it would be too hurtful and not worth the effort?

HIM

HER

If you had a problem with me and we took care of it, would there be anything left that would bother you within the next month (like additional issues coming up)? Please explain.

HIM

HER

Am I too critical, judgmental, unfair, negative, or controlling in my word choices or attitudes toward others? If so, please share any example.

HIM

HER

If we were to win the lottery, what would be your first purchase and why would it be that item?

HIM

HER

What do you think I am most self-conscious of, and why?

HIM

HER

Do you think meeting me changed your life (if yes, in what way)?

HIM

HER

Are there any very important times of year or wonderful memories that should come up soon that "we" need to prepare for and enjoy together?

HIM

HER

Question:

HIM

HER

Question:

HIM

HER

Question:

HIM

HER

Question:

HIM

HER

Question:

HIM

HER

Question:

HIM

HER

Question:

HIM

HER

Question:

HIM

HER

Question:

HIM

HER

Question:

HIM

Please Leave a Review

Do you enjoy this book? What do you like about this book? How do you think other readers can benefit from this book?

Please spare a few minutes to leave an honest review on Amazon. Your thoughts and review are important, and you will help to make a difference in someone else's life.

Thank you!

www.ingramcontent.com/pod-product-compliance
Lightning Source LLC
Chambersburg PA
CBHW081336120626

46546CB00011B/3374